Growing Up Humming

Written & Photographed By Mike Spinak

Growing Up Humming © 2013 by Mike Spinak
Text Copyright © 2012 Mike Spinak
Photo Copyright © 2012 Mike Spinak
Library of Congress Control Number: 2013906761

All rights reserved. No part of this book may be reproduced or transmitted in any form or by any means, electronic or mechanical, including photocopying, recording, or by any information storage and retrieval system, without permission in writing from the copyright holder.

Published in North Las Vegas, Nevada by Mike Spinak
Telephone: (831) 325-6917
Email: mikespinak@gmail.com
Manufactured in the United States of America

Thank you,

Aaron Spinak, Alan Shapiro, Ann Hardy, Barry Blanchard, Bella Hopewell, Billy Wilson, Cedar Hopewell, Christina Rollo, Ed Sweeney, Elizabeth Hahn, Garbiela Zavadilova, Jennifer Hardy, Jessica Rae Chipera, Joanne Manaster, Kasia Hopewell, Larry Spinak, Lee Daniels, Mara Acoma, Michael Frye, Monique Yates, Norm Hardy, Quinn Mazurek, Renée Snodgrass, Ron Wolf, Tal Thompson, and everyone who pledged funds for this book through Kickstarter.

Without you, this book would not have been possible.

This is a mother Anna's hummingbird. She's looking around to make sure nobody is watching. She doesn't want predators to find her chicks.

These are her two chicks. They live in this nest on top of a seed pod. Their mother made the nest out of spiderwebs, lichens, feathers, and leaves.

The chicks are fifteen days old and thirteen days old. They hatched from eggs about the size of peas. At birth, they couldn't open their eyes. Their black and pink skin was bare. They slept almost all the time. They were so little that their heads were below the edge of the nest.

After two weeks of growth, now their heads rise above the edge. Their bodies fill the nest. Their eyes are open. Their feathers are starting to come in and cover their bare skin. Even the tips of their wing feathers are starting to poke through the feather sheaths. But they still have bald pink patches on their chests, and their beaks are still short and yellowish. They won't be grown up for another week.

The chicks need to eat a lot to grow up so fast. Mother hummingbird flies away from the nest to gather food while the chicks rest. She drinks flower nectar and eats small insects.

She comes back to feed them every fifteen to thirty minutes. When she comes, the chicks wake up and become active. They fully open their eyes, and lift their heads.

Mother hummingbird stands on the edge of the nest. She puts her beak down one chick's throat and brings back up the insects and nectar she stored in her stomach. Then she does the same with the other chick.

Feeding chicks this way is called "regurgitation."

By regurgitating, Mother breaks down the food in her own stomach, before feeding the chicks. The chicks' stomachs aren't yet developed enough for them to fully break down the food for themselves.

The feedings only last five or ten seconds. Then Mother flies away again.

The next day, the sixteen and fourteen day old chicks' beaks are much longer. When they grow up, their beaks will be almost twice as long as this, again. Their beaks will also become black and very pointy. For now, they are still mostly yellow, and still have hooked tips.

The hooked beak tip is left over from when the chick hatched. It is called an "egg tooth," because the unborn chick uses it to peck its way out of the egg.

The wing feathers are coming in. Yesterday, just the tips of the wing feathers poked through the sheaths. Today, these feathers are poking out far enough to start to unfurl.

The chicks are much more wakeful and aware, now. They sit up, open eyed, and open their mouths to ask their mother for food. This is called "gaping."

Unfurling Wing Feathers

Wing Feather Sheaths

The chicks are now almost as big as their mother. The feathering on their bodies filled out overnight, covering their skin much more. The bigger the chicks get, and the more their feathers come in, the more the chicks can stay warm by themselves.

Keeping themselves warm is called "thermoregulating." When they can thermoregulate, their mother spends less time on the nest warming them, and more time gathering food for them.

Anna's hummingbird fathers don't help raise chicks, so Mother needs as much time as she can get to feed two large chicks all by herself.

Two days later, at eighteen days old, Big Sister hummingbird no longer looks like a baby bird. She's now more adolescent than infant.

Her beak is darker, is losing the egg tooth, and is now perhaps two-thirds as long as her mother's. Her feathering covers her body well in all but a few places, and no longer looks scraggly. The first hints of green iridescence are visible in her feathers on her shoulders and back. Her bits of fluffy baby down now stand out sharply from her adult feathers.

She's now so large that she tends to sit on the nest, rather than in the nest. She's much more alert and aware of her surroundings, especially paying attention to the activities of the egrets and herons nesting above.

The next day, Big Sister is developing new behaviors.
These include stretching her wings –

– tongue flicking –

– preening –

– and a little bit of experimental wing flapping. At this point, it is perhaps more like wing waving.

Two days later, at twenty-one days old and nineteen days old, both chicks are so large that they not only sit on top of the nest, rather than in the nest, they also spend most of their time facing opposite directions, to stay out of each other's way.

At this stage, Little Sister often seems to mimic her older sister.

Big Sister now ventures out to the edge of the nest, and perches there. She's twenty-one days old, and about ready to fly off.

Big Sister is eager to fly. She stands on the edge of the nest and flaps her wings furiously. She flaps her wings for a while; then rests; then tries again. She does this all day long.

When the night comes, she flies for the first time, leaving the nest forever. Now she follows Mother hummingbird through the trees and meadows, learning how to find food and avoid danger.

The day after Big Sister left, Little Sister is twenty days old. Mother wants Little Sister to fly, too. It will be easier for Mother with both chicks following her, than with one chick flying and one chick still on the nest. To try to get Little Sister to fly away, Mother made the nest colder and less comfortable by removing some material from it, overnight.

But Little Sister isn't ready to fly, yet. Her wings aren't developed enough. She still has bare wing feather sheaths where the wing feathers haven't yet grown in to cover them.

Mother tries another way to convince Little Sister to fly out.

She flies in, then – instead of immediately feeding Little Sister, as in the past – she waits a few inches away and softly calls Little Sister to come out of the nest to her.

Little Sister doesn't budge. Mother leans in and feeds her. She now has to feed Little Sister more from the side while standing on a branch. Because Little Sister has grown so tall, Mother can no longer easily feed her directly downward, while standing on the edge of the nest.

Mother now feeds Little Sister more from the side for safety reasons, too. Little Sister's beak is so long that she could accidentally poke Mother in the eye or throat, as she eagerly bounces and tugs during feedings. This is another reason that Little Sister must soon leave.

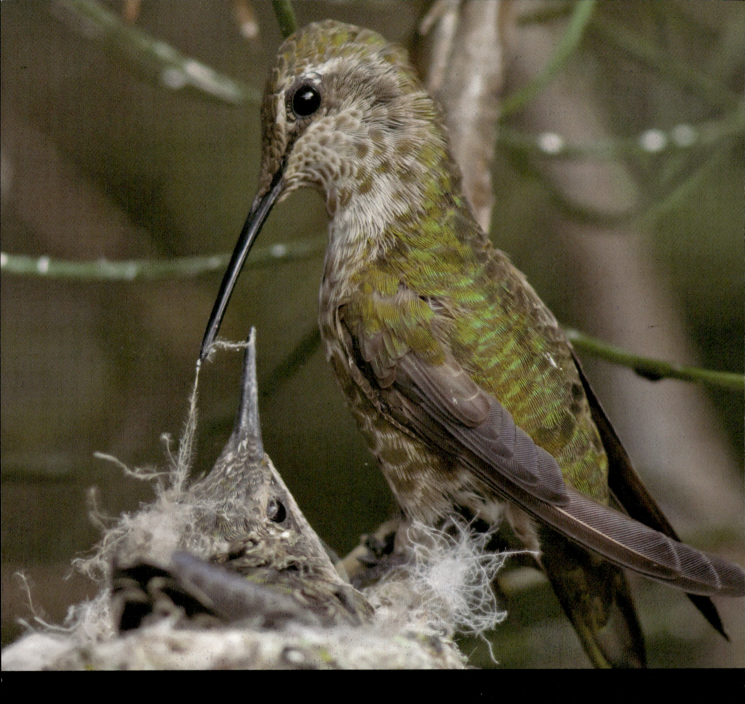

Mother's next step to get Little Sister to fly is to pluck away all of Little Sister's down feathers. Little Sister is so big that she can thermoregulate as an adult, without the additional insulation.

Now it's more important for her to be ready for her new life in flight.

Birds flap their wings to move through the air a lot like people paddle their arms and kick their legs to move through the water. Just like a big coat would cause drag through the water and make it harder for someone to swim, Little Sister's down feathers would drag through the air and make it harder to fly – so the fluffy baby feathers have to go.

Without the fluffy down feathers, Little Sister will be more "aerodynamic." Aerodynamic means shaped so air flows easily around her when she moves through it, without dragging against her.

Little Sister stays put, despite having her down feathers plucked. She flutters her wings a bit, but she's just not ready to fly.

The next day, Little Sister looks much more adult.

She's getting quite large. When she sits up, she looks very oversized for her little nest. The nest can't shelter her anymore, so it's time to leave.

Little Sister explores more, now. She watches everything going on around the nest, reaches out for everything within touching distance, and – most of all –

– tastes everything nearby. This is part of the learning process for a chick about to fly. She's discovering what is food and what isn't.

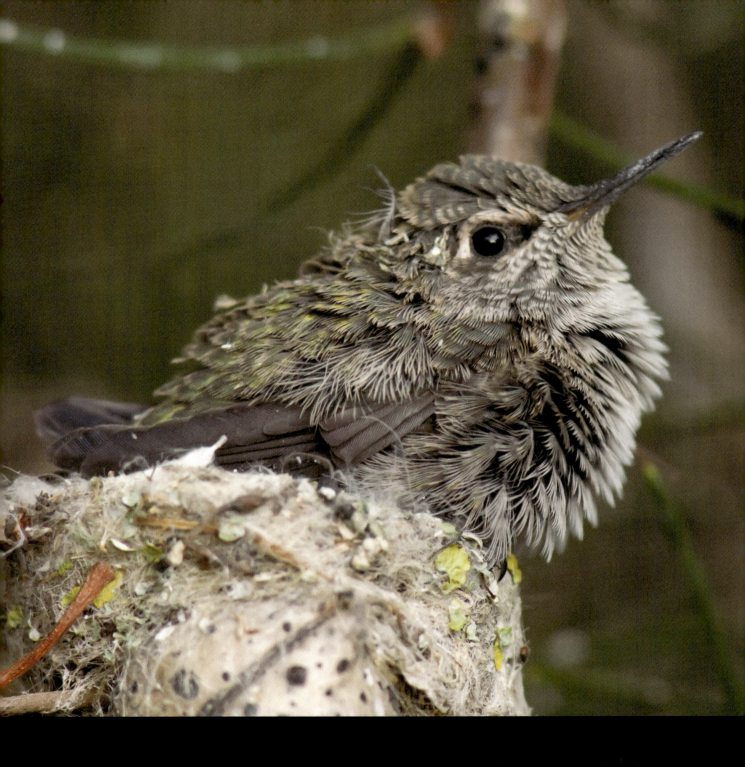

Like Big Sister had done, Little Sister now spends a lot of time ruffling her feathers.

After ruffling her feathers, she preens them.

After preening, she also spends much of her time stretching her wings. Although some small patches of bare pink skin show through at the bases of the wings, Little Sister acts ready to fly.

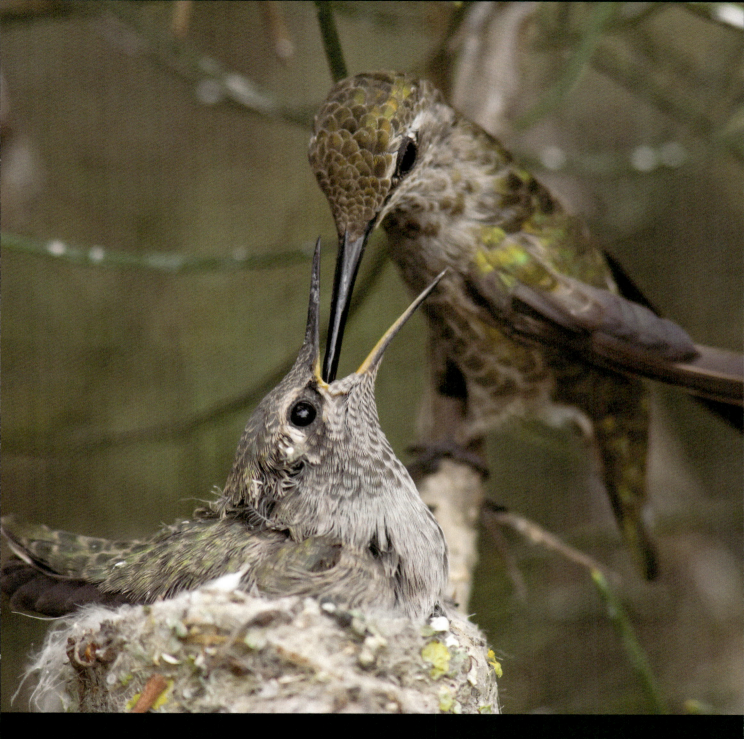

Now, when Mother comes in to feed Little Sister –

– she sticks around for a few minutes after the feeding, and presses right down on top of Little Sister while flapping her wings. Maybe this teaches Little Sister how to flap her own wings. Or maybe it stimulates Little Sister's flying instincts. Perhaps both.

Energized by a belly full of regurgitated insects and nectar, and perhaps following Mother's example, Little Sister practices flapping her wings shortly after each feeding. Like a toddler learning to walk, the first tries are a little wobbly.

Soon Little Sister learns to stabilize herself, keeping her head and body steady while only her wings move.

She stands on the edge of the nest for long flapping sessions, while rotating around and around.

During the night, Little Sister flies off. She joins Mother and Big Sister to fly through the trees and meadows, and to learn how to find food and avoid danger.

Soon, the chicks will fly far away from Mother and start lives of their own.

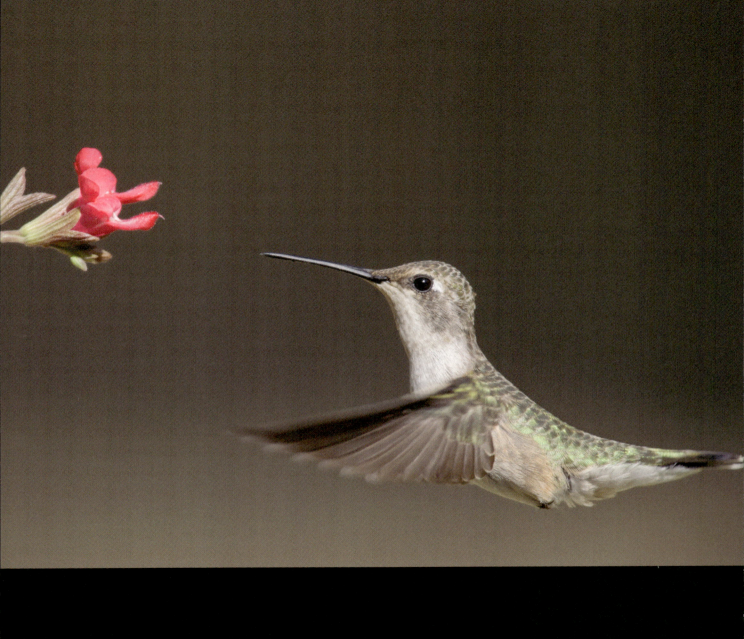

They'll find food for themselves.

Some day, they'll raise their own chicks, just like their mother raised them.

The End

Anna's Hummingbird Facts

- Anna's hummingbirds were named by Rene Primevere Lesson for Anna De Belle Massena, Duchess of Rivoli.

- A flock of Anna's hummingbirds is called a bouquet, a glittering, a shimmer, a hover, or a tune.

- They normally weigh a little less than a nickel, but may fatten up to almost double their weight before migration.

- They eat up to half their weight each day.

- They are more carnivorous than most hummingbirds, and they like to feed by plucking all the trapped insects off of spider webs.

- Their hearts beat over 1,200 times per minute while flying, but slow down to about 50 beats per minute overnight.

- Anna's hummingbirds have such small legs that they can't walk.

- They usually flap their wings about 50 times per second.

- Hummingbirds are the only kind of birds which can hover in place, fly forward, backward, straight sideways, straight up or down, and can even fly upside down.

- Their normal flight speed is about 25 miles per hour, with a maximum flight speed of about 40 miles per hour.